For a day in thy courts *is* better than a thousand. I had rather be a doorkeeper in the house of my God, than to dwell in the tents of wickedness.

Psalm 84:10 KJV

From the Heart of the Author

I started out wanting this book to be what I wanted it to be. Now, I thank God for wisdom to know that it had to be what GOD wanted it to be. I started out wanting it to be a 365 day devotional. Well, here's a truth that most people don't want to admit - they normally don't make it 365 days before they get distracted, discouraged or disengaged. I know this to be true from experience.

The Lord spoke to me and said "daughter, you must feed My people the way I instruct you to feed them because I know what they have need of. I know how much or how little they can handle." This time, I didn't talk back. I simply accepted the fact that my plan had to fail because God's plan had to succeed. His plan will yield His results and my responsibility is to follow His lead, release the Word of the Lord and let Him do the work. I also accepted the fact that even though it's a 60 day devotional, far from 365 days- it's what God has graced me to produce. I'd rather follow the cloud than to go my own way and cause others to miss what God is doing or is about to do. I dare not be a hindrance or a hold up for God's people receiving what He has prepared for them. I wasn't planning on finishing or releasing this book because I didn't think I'd make it. More than that, I didn't even feel motivated to do it. But God, who is sovereign, had a plan that He planned long before I had a plan. I had to trust the God of the plan and believe that His will was being done. I encourage you to follow the plan of God and the peace of God. Operate in the grace that He has given you for your life, family, business and/or ministry. Stop talking back to God so much and be quicker to move in obedience to His voice. Obedience births blessings for you and others. You don't know who is waiting on you and you may not even know what they need. Let the wisdom of the Lord guide you because God knows! Trust Him to use you to minister, encourage, empower and strengthen those that He has called you to. Lastly, when the plan of God is revealed to you, trust the God of the plan even if you're unsure about the plan! ~ LaTrice

Day 1

Your WHY is Important!

You must remember that while man looks at the outer appearance, God looks at and judges your heart. The reference scripture teaches and reminds you that you must share Jesus so that others can enjoy Him and have the same joy that you experience because of your relationship with Him.

It is important to remember that the same reasons that you need Jesus are the same reasons that others need him as well.

It's a good time to ask yourself -why do I do what I do?

Even in sharing Christ, you must know your "why." Christ wants your "why" to be based on the right motives in all things that you do. As you go through your day, examine your motives for sharing Christ and for all things that you do in the name of Christ.

Your "WHY" is important! Your "WHY" should lift up Jesus and glorify Him. As you journey through life, check your motives before you make your moves. As you share the good news of Jesus Christ, share it so that the name of Jesus will be made known and others will be introduced to the love, grace and hope that you have experienced. As you go throughout this day, don't forget to check your motives and make sure your "why" is pure in the sight of the Lord.

Scripture for Meditation: 1 John 1:3-4 Message Bible

Day 2

Walk in the Light!

Jesus is the light and He wants to fellowship with you! If you confess your sin, He is faithful and just to forgive your sins and cleanse you from all unrighteousness. Confession opens the door to forgiveness and righteousness. What do you need to confess to God today?

You should take a few moments daily to confess sin to the Father regardless of how small or large you believe them to be. You should pray that His light will drive out all darkness in you. Light and darkness cannot dwell together. Light will always drive out darkness. Jesus is The Light that can drive out all darkness from your life.

Do you know what areas that you need the Light of Jesus to shine in? Is it your thoughts? Maybe it's how you talk? Is it how you treat others? Where is the darkness in you that needs The Light?

The truth is that you need The Light every day of your life in every area. I encourage you to be thankful for His faithfulness toward you and being just to forgive and cleanse you. Embrace every opportunity to fellowship with the Savior! As you go throughout this day, receive God's forgiveness, pray for strength to continually walk in the light and allow His light to shine through you!

Scripture for Meditation: 1 John 1:5-10 New King James Version

Day 3

Jesus, Our Help!

Today's scripture gives us insight into how God sees us. He sees us as His little children that He instructs and protects. As an adult, you may say that you are grown men and women but for God to look at us as His little ones that need to be continually instructed and cared for should make our hearts smile. We grow in age, we mature spiritually yet God continually wants to care for us and instruct us so that He can HELP US! Secondly, He instructs us so that we'll stay away from sin. He tells us that IF we do sin and if we're honest when we do, there is someone to plead (to argue our case, to cry out for us, to present us before God) before the Father. How loving is God that WHEN we sin, He strategically put Jesus in place to HELP US not condemn us.

Here is a question to ask yourself today- Am I really IN Christ? The scripture is clear that you have to look within yourself. It isn't about comparing yourself to others, it's not about what you have or don't have but it's about what's going on IN you. It's about are you doing what God says? It's just that simple. Am I saying that we'll always get it right? Nope! All have sinned (past tense) and fall short (present tense) of the glory of God. But, beloved, are you really striving to do what God tells you to do? Are you striving to live as close to His word as possible? As the scripture teaches, anyone who says he is a Christian should live as Christ did. Simply said, you should do what God said because Christ did. As you go throughout this day, remember that Jesus is your help.

Scripture for Meditation: 1 John 2: 1-6 The Living Bible

Day 4

The Time To Get Right Is Now!

There is a reason that God continues to send you warnings. He's even sending warnings through the manifestation of His word. What is written in the bible is showing up in the land that you live in. But how long will Gods own people, not those of the world, but Gods people continue to ignore Him? How long will you continue to walk in your own way? How long will you stay in the places that you know you've been in way too long?

The mouth pieces of God are crying out unto you. The evidence that Gods Word is true is happening all around us. It's expected that those who don't accept the Lord and His word will not heed the warning but those of you who know Him, claim to love Him, and are serving Him- the question is HOW LONG?

The prophet Micah's warning is clear- God is about to take the witness stand against you! Beloved, what charge will God make against you? What accusation will He have against you? The Lord IS COMING! As you go through out this day, make a conscious decision and effort to heed the warning and get your life right now!

Scripture for Meditation: Micah 1:2 & 8-9 Message Bible

Day 5

God Knows His Plan! Commit It To Him!

Beloved, it is the Lords desire that you succeed. He has orchestrated a great plan for your lives that was predestined before the foundation of this world. He understands that you have great vision, plans and goals because it was Him that allowed you to see these things in your spirit man. God is calling for you to submit those visions, plans and goals to HIM. Because HE is the Master of those plans, He can show you how to work the vision, write the business plans and He can ensure that they do what He planned for them to do.

There really is no success outside of that which God allows. Regardless of what the world wants you to think concerning success, true success comes when God's desires are your desires, when His righteousness is your righteousness and His plans are your plans. I urge you to follow the plan of God, commit it all to Him and believe to see the success that only God can bring.

God knows the plan better than you ever will. You should always be mindful that His ways are not your ways, His thoughts are not your thoughts but they are higher. Take joy in knowing that what God has planned for you is higher than what you've conceived in your mind. To experience HIS success, you must commit it all to HIM.

You must commit all of you, all that you have, all that you desire and even all that you're to the Lord and His promise is that you will succeed. As you go through this day, consciously commit your God given goals, aspirations, plans and dreams to God and allow Him in prayer and receive His instruction to activate and navigate through them.

Scripture for Meditation: Proverbs 16:3 Jeremiah 29:11
New International Version

Day 6

Show Up In Me, Jesus!

Have you ever prayed – show up in me, Jesus?

You should always pray that the faith that you hold in common with other believers shows up in the good things that you do and that people will recognize Christ in all of it.

Your reminder today is that in everything that you do - it's not about you. Your ultimate goal should always be for Christ to be seen.

It's not about making your name known but making Christ known among the people.

Many people have heard His name but you, His blood bought children have the opportunity to do the good in this world that will cause people to SEE Him. You can do more than just talk about Him, you can show Him to the world. You can accomplish this through your actions of love, generosity, kindness and grace.

Two good questions to ponder as you go through this day are:

Is the good that you're doing showing up and showing Christ?

How can I cause Christ to be seen more in my life?

Scripture for Meditation: Philemon 1:4-7 Message Bible

Day 7

Take The Limits Off of Yourself!

God is limitless and because of His strength power, the things in this life that you can accomplish are limitless as well. Often times, you may limit yourself because of your past. You may think that because things didn't work out the way you wanted or hoped before that they won't work out again. It's time to put our fears and negative thoughts to death and live in the truth that God has prescribed for our lives. That truth is we can do ALL things THROUGH CHRIST!

You are also limiting yourself by trying to do things within your own strength. Alone, you are not strong enough. Alone, you are not intelligent enough. Alone, you are not capable of achieving the success and greatness that God has planned for us BUT THROUGH CHRIST! Today is the day that you should development the mindset - BUT THROUGH CHRIST!

Because of Christ, you don't have to attempt anything alone. You don't have to plan alone. You don't have to live alone. You don't have to start your business alone. You don't have to carry your ministry alone! God already has the plan for your life!

All you have to do is seek Him for the direction and follow the instructions!

You can do it! Whatever IT is! You can do ALL! Whatever your ALL is - THROUGH CHRIST the plan for your life will succeed! Always remember that you can do nothing without Christ but you can do all things through Him and with Him.

Scripture for Meditation: Philippians 4:13 New International Version

Day 8

Don't Give Up!

Have you ever felt like the more you did right, the more things seemed to go wrong? Or the more you strived for excellence, sometimes it felt like you couldn't accomplish anything you set out to do? Every time you tried to do good- there was always something that happened opposite of what you're reaching for?

Would you believe that those were simply distractions that were meant to keep you from reaching your goal? They were meant to cause you to take your eyes off of Christ and divert your attention to the problem instead of the promise. Beloved, be encouraged - the promise is still yours.

The enemy wants to discourage you and make you believe that you can't accomplish the goals that you've set. That's his job. He wants you to think that your dreams will not come to pass but you must not give up now. You just may be on the brink of everything that you've worked and prayed for.

I encourage you to do as Apostle Paul said - forget those things which are behind you and reach forward! Press toward the mark of the prize of the high calling in Christ Jesus.

Don't give up because there is a blessing in your pressing and a reward for your faithfulness. There's more looking for you and the best is yet to come! Giving up shouldn't be your option when winning is your promise!

Scripture for Meditation: Philippians 3:13-14 New Living Translation

Day 9

That's Not Your Battle to Fight!

There is an old song that I love to sing that says be still God will fight your battles. God will fight your battles if you just be still!

I want to encourage you that no matter what the battle may be; whether it appears to be in your home or family, at your job, in your finances, in your emotions and feelings, in your mind or within yourself - you have the solemn promise of God that He will fight for you.

You must always remember that every trial that you encounter and tribulation that you endure- it's not your battle even though it seems to be raging against you. The battle really belongs to the Lord because the enemy is not really against you but the GOD in you!

Every attack against you is against God. Remember the least that is done unto us is done unto Him. God has counted us worthy in this time of battle to be a vessel that He will work through yet He's given us promise that He will fight for us.

As our Scripture for Meditation for today says, don't be afraid or dismayed. What looks like a problem to you is really a promise about to be fulfilled from God. Don't even consider putting your hands on this adversity that you're dealing with. It's not yours, it's God's.

You don't have to talk your way out of it, manipulate your way out of it, worry your way through it or stress out about it. The promises of God are yes and amen so be encouraged and know that He's fighting for you.

The beauty of this battle that you don't have to fight is that you'll still get to enjoy the benefits of the victory!

Scripture for Meditation: 2 Chronicles 20:15 New International Version

Day 10

Jesus Loves You!

Often it is taken for granted what the love of Jesus means for you. If you'll take just a few moments to remember John 3:16, you'll be reminded of the magnitude of that love.

I don't believe that many of you can imagine willingly giving up your ONLY son or child to save a world that may or may not accept your love or your sacrifice. But the love of Jesus for you is unselfish and selfless. It spoke volumes without even speaking words. His actions proved His love.

Take comfort knowing that Gods' love for you drove Him to redemptive action for you. Jesus loved you so much that He bowed His head and gave up His Spirit. When Jesus could have saved His own life, he chose to save yours. When Jesus could have shut the mouth of the naysayers without dying, He stayed in the process and allowed His Father to have His perfect work in and through Him. The song writer was right, Jesus came and did it just for me and you.

Where ever you are today in life- God loves you. If you are backslidden - God is married to the backslider but you do not have to stay in the place that you're in. The love of God is redemptive for all who will receive it. He's waiting with open arms and abundant love to receive you back. If you've never accepted Christ as your Savior - He loves you. When He died, He died for you too. He's waiting for you to receive Him into your heart.

Whatever your lot today, know that Jesus loves you! He loves you and that is more than enough!

Scripture for Meditation: John 3:16, John 19:30, Romans 5:8
King James Version

Day 11

Greater Is Coming!

Whatever you are dealing with, especially in the places that you feel like you're suffering - they don't compare to what God is doing in you! Your trials are preparing you for the promise that God has on you and the potential that is in you!

Paul said that your suffering is about what's going to be revealed IN you! It's not about what's going to happen to us or for us but what God is going to manifest in us.

I am reminded of the scripture that says Greater is HE that is IN me that he that is in the world. When God gets ready to reveal the Glory in you- can you imagine what that will look like? Do you know that the glory carrier, Christ Jesus, is living on the inside of you?

His glory is incomparable and indescribable.

What looks like it's working against you at this present time, in this present day, will be incomparable and indescribable when His glory is revealed in you!

Everything happening now is working for the greater that's coming forth in you!

As you go throughout this day, encourage yourself and remind yourself that the "NOW" trouble is necessary to reveal the promised glory. I believe that gospel artist Vickie Winans sang a song that said- *"Your Latter Will Be Greater."* Encourage yourself and believe God that greater is coming.

Scripture for Meditation: Romans 8:18 New International Version; 1 John 4:4 King James Version

Day 12

Consider YOU!

Have you taken the time to consider you? Often you can see or pinpoint things externally that may be hindering you or have the potential to hinder you but the Lord wants you to look internally.

The things that are working against you internally will hinder you more than anything externally. Have you honestly looked at you and examined your ways to make sure it's not YOU that's holding YOU back? It is possible.

It has been said that you can be your own worst critics but you can also be your own worst enemy. Everything that's wrong isn't because of someone else. It isn't always because the enemy has launched out against you.

Sometimes it's the war that is raging within yourself that causes setbacks, losses and more.

If you're wondering what may be wrong in your life - consider "your ways?" If you're baffled about why some things have or have not happened - consider "your ways". You can't take "you" out of the equation of your life. You must first consider your own ways before you shift the blame or reasoning onto other people and things!

Do a self-check **today**. It's worth it and more importantly you and your vision for life are worth it.

Scripture for Meditation: Haggai 1:5 New International Version

Day 13

God- Giver of Dreams and Visions!

It's time to seek God for HIS answer and approval. Too often you may seek the very limited opinion of man but it is God that has the unlimited knowledge, revelation and power to make all of the dreams and visions that He has given you come to pass?

Stop limiting Him to tangible things that you can buy for yourself. He wants to give you exceedingly and abundantly above that.

Houses, cars and possessions are good and God has no problem with you having them but the problem is when the THINGS HAVE YOU! Some of us have gotten GOT by the things.

You've also limited God and His Word by not fully realizing that "things" includes His wisdom that you could never afford to pay for but desperately need. It includes His power that you need to accomplish His purpose for your lives. It also includes His Spirit who you need to live through you so that you be the greater that He has ordained for you.

You can't live greater without the greater one living in you!

Beloved, God wants to pour out these "things" on you and in you but you're seeking in the wrong areas. Stop looking for God to hand you keys to a new temporary blessing when God wants to pour out His eternal blessings on you. Get in the posture of seeking God for your dreams and visions and you'll see HIS "things" manifest.

Friends, family and co-laborers are good to share your dreams and visions with but God is the manufacturer of them. HE alone has the answers and the power to cause you to possess them. Today - See the giver!

Scripture for Meditation: Matthew 6:33 King James Version

Day 14

Avail Yourself to God!

The encouragement for you today is to avail yourself to God.

Life challenges have a tendency to pull you in multiple directions and sometimes you feel like giving up. There are times when you simply want God to take it all away, relieve the pain immediately and give you instant relief.

Today, I challenge you to avail yourself to God and His will for your life. There is no promise that it will be easy but the promise is that it will work for your good!

When Jesus prayed the prayer in the Garden of Eden, He was on his way to Calvary. He knew the certain death that He was facing. Despite those facts, He still availed Himself to His Father.

It is important to learn to follow the example of Jesus. No matter what you're facing and regardless of how difficult the climb may seem to you, be willing to avail yourself to God.

God can do more with you and your life than you could ever do alone! As you encounter people, places and things that challenge your strength and your faith, remember what Jesus did. He availed Himself to the Father and won the victory! So shall you!

Scripture for Meditation: Luke 22:42 New International Version

Day 15

Always Pray!

Prayer is essential to your life as a Christian. You cannot live the abundant life without effective prayer. I know the world wants you to believe that you can. However the scriptures that teach you about the necessity, importance and the benefit of prayer.

You should pray about everything! It doesn't matter how small you think it is, God has an answer for it. Whatever your plight is today, commit it to the Lord in prayer.

And don't forget that prayer is more than talking to God, it also requires listening! After you've worshiped the Lord, offered your praise to Him and lifted up your concerns, I urge you to listen for His reply.

In prayer, God gives you wisdom, direction, encouragement, strength and more. Healing takes place through prayer. Deliverance is birthed through prayer. In prayer, miracles began to manifest.

If you will know or remember Peter's story, it was while they were praying for His release that Peter showed up at the door. God had already answered.

I submit to you that while you are praying, the answer is on the way to you!

Prayer is critical every day! It is your weapon of war that guarantees you endless victory.

Scripture for Meditation: 1 Thessalonians 5:7 King James Version; Acts 12:5-17 New King James Version

Day 16

Watch Your Words!

From the fruit of your mouth and the harvest of your heart- that's what you'll see in your life. Some of you need to revisit some of the things that you've said over the course of life. You may find that what you've said is what you've seen.

It's a good time to decide how you're going to be filled and satisfied. You should make up our mind that it is going to be different going forward.

You have to change what you speak, especially about yourself. Too often people are concerned about what others are saying about them. God wants you to concern yourself with what about what YOU are saying about you?

The tongue has the power of life and death so you must be careful how you use it. If you don't want to see it, then you should not speak it. Some of you are killing your own lives with the words that you say. You are killing your own dreams with the words of self-doubt that you speak. The scripture also says those who love it will EAT its' fruit.

Beloved, when you change what you speak, you will change what you eat!

As I said in the beginning, from the fruit of our mouth and the harvest of your heart, that's what you'll see in our lives. This is a good day to decide what you want to see.

Scripture for Meditation: Proverbs 18:20-21 New International Version

Day 17

Have You Denied Him?

Today would be a good day to evaluate your life and do a self-check. It's not really a question of have you denied Jesus but how many times have you done it and in how many ways?

Have your words denied that He is your Savior? What about your actions? In the face of adversity has doubt caused you to deny Jesus? In the face of opposition, have your responses caused you to deny Jesus?

Consider this today - is your life denying Christ? Are you speaking about Him, benefiting from Him yet your way of living still denies Him? Consider carefully.

Don't deny Him today! Present yourselves a living sacrifice, holy, acceptable unto God which is your reasonable service to God.

David said acknowledge the Lord in all of your ways and He will direct your path. Do you know that means to acknowledge the Lord even if your ways have not been pleasing to Him? Do you know that He wants you to acknowledge Him in everything?

In every area of your life, make a conscious effort to never deny the Savior but to acknowledge Him and your need of Him.

Scripture for Meditation: John 18: 17 & 25-27 New International Version
Romans 12:1 King James Version; Proverbs 3:6 King James Version

Day 18

Make Room For His Word!

Beloved, God wants to enlarge your capacity to receive from Him.

It is necessary that you make room for God's Word! Many people talk about being free in Jesus but have you considered that in order to remain free you must make room for His Word?

The more you read Gods' Word, the more you will know that you need to make MORE room! Some of you are reading, studying and praying yet there is still MORE that God wants you to have of Him.

You may be a person that reads scripture sporadically or when you feel that you have time but when will we make time? It is necessary to set aside some specific time and then make room for what the Word is saying to you?

Do you have room for the correction that is in God's Word like you have room for the encouragement? Do you have room for Gods' Word when it calls you out of sin and into holy living? Do you have room for Gods' Word when it urges you to put away the things of the flesh and go after the things of the spirit?

I urge you today to make room for Gods' Word. His Word will improve the quality of your life. It will increase you in every area of your life. If you'd only make room for His Word, then His Word would truly make room in your life. Make a decision today, to make time and make room for God's Word in you and in your life!

Scripture for Meditation: John 8:34-38 New Living Translation

Day 19

Not Yet!

God wants you to learn to follow the examples of Jesus! You must not allow people who don't even really believe in you to push you into places and things before it's time! You must be in relationship with Jesus so that you will know when it's your turn and your time!

Don't be swayed by the opinions and pushes of people to move in a time that is not yours. Don't allow counterfeit supporters to cause you to go into the birthing room too soon or leap into a vision too early. Remember that Habakkuk said the vision is for an appointed time!

You must follow the example of Jesus. Sometimes you have to say- my time is not YET! That may mean that others will go before you. It may mean that others will leap first or jump in before you.

It doesn't mean that you aren't going- it only means, NOT YET!

Beloved, sometimes 'not yet' is Gods' protection for you.

I encourage you to do it in Gods' timing and not man. Follow Gods' leading and not man. Your time is fully coming. I pray that you'll wait on God to move you into it and don't allow man to push you prematurely! Premature births can cause unnecessary loss.

Scripture for Meditation: John 7:1-8 New Living Translation;
Habakkuk 2:3 King James Version

Day 20

Who Are You Trusting?

I remember listening to John chapter two one day on my drive in to work. The last verses caused me to rewind. Both literally and mentally. I had to ask myself the question, do you KNOW who you are entrusting yourself to?

The scripture says that just because the people believed His name because of the signs He performed, He still didn't entrust His life to them. When I read the Message Bible version, it said that Jesus could see right through them. He could see how untrustworthy they were.

Now, clearly you aren't Jesus but He has given you a spirit of discernment to see the spirit of a person but have you used it?

Do you know these people that have attached themselves to you? Do you know the motives of these people? Maybe they have attached to you because of where they may think God is taking you or what He's doing in you?

It may be time to consider who you have entrusted your life to. Not only your physical life but emotionally and mentally as well. Most importantly, who have you entrusted your spiritual life to?

I challenge you today to rewind and take a closer look at who you've trusted. Ask the Lord to help you see them for who He knows that they really are and not who you want or hope for them to be!

Scripture for Meditation: John 2:23-25 New International Version; Message Bible

Day 21

God Foreknew!

Beloved, do you know that you were in the foreknowledge of God? You were not an after-thought. You were not created because God didn't have anything else to do or to create. You were always on the mind of God and God always had a plan for you.

Don't allow the enemy to make you think that you're only in that place or working at that job or living in that house or preaching in that place because somebody else couldn't do it. The devil is a lie concerning you. God's word is still true. God FOREKNEW you and what you would do in His Kingdom. He planned who you would be and how He would use you.

Lift your head up, beloved, because you were already chosen. Square your shoulders because what God KNEW about you then is STILL what He knows about you now!

Be encouraged, you are there because God foreknew you. You hold that position, that title, that mantle, that job, and live that life because God foreknew you. Let that bless your life! It's not a mistake at all. It is God ordained. It is God known. It is God breathed. Not only are you called to this but you are chosen!

Scripture for Meditation: 1 Peter 1:1-2 New Living Translation

Day 22

It Has Already Began!

The day is coming when you'll have it all - life healed and whole. The future starts now! You don't have to wait to live better, be happy, have peace, or to have joy- the future starts now and everything that is coming in your future starts now! God is watching over you. He's waiting to give you every good thing.

Everything that God planned for you has already began!

Although you are waiting and working and believing and trusting, God has already put the future that He destined for you into motion. It's comforting to know that in everything that you may be encountering right now, the good and the bad, God is keeping careful watch over you and your future!

What does that mean? God has His eyes and His hands on you and the things that He has planned for you. He is divinely and strategically aligning things to work out for your good. That's why no weapon formed against you shall be able to prosper. God isn't going to let anything or anyone hinder the future that He has already started working on for you!

Beloved, I pray that you'll get excited about what God is already doing. If you are unsure, you should be reassured that it will come to pass. God is watching your future to make sure nothing harms it, nothing hinders it and nothing keeps you from it!

Get excited and reignite your expectation because it has already started!

Scripture for Meditation: 1 Peter 1:1-5 Message Bible

Day 23

One Day She Got Herself Together!

Will today be the day that you get yourself together? God know that you've been dealt some hard blows. Things may not have worked out exactly as you may have wished but now is a good time to regroup and get yourself together.

In the first chapter of Ruth, Naomi was left with her two daughter in laws and the clothes on her back as she described it. She felt as if she had nothing more to offer them and that she never would.

Has this ever been your plight? Have you ever felt like you didn't have anything to offer those around you? Have you ever felt like you'd never be able to give them what they needed or desired?

Just as Naomi was a help to Ruth, you are the answer that someone needs. What's IN you is what someone else will need for the next phase of their life. Even though life may be turning you upside down right now, make a decision to get yourself together because somebody is going to need you. Somebody is going to need what's in you!

I encourage you - Get Yourself Together! It's going to be a blessing to someone else and YOU!

Scripture for Meditation: Ruth 1:6-7 Message Bible

Day 24

You Can!

God wants you to focus on what you can do instead of what you feel that you can't do.

It's time to take God at His Word literally. Philippians 4:13 states "I can do ALL things through Christ who strengthens me!" The only limitations on the things that you can accomplish are set by your limited thinking. You must take off the mindset that will hinder you. You may encounter obstacles or roadblocks but it doesn't change the fact that you still have what you need to do whatever God has called you to do.

Fill your heart up with what God says about you today and speak what God says about you. Don't speak your circumstances and situations. When you do that, you give them power over you. Take charge of your life. Take charge of your destiny and assignment. Believe without doubting that whatever things you've been assigned to - Christ has enough strength for you! Apostle Paul reminds you that God's grace is sufficient in 2nd Corinthians. Beloved, the grace of God is working on your behalf. You can do what God says you can do. You can be what God says you can be. You can have what God says you can have. You can go where God says you can go.

The challenge to you today is: 1. Commit your plans to the Lord. 2. Speak the Word of God concerning yourself. Remember that you can do all things through Christ who strengthens you. 3. Believe God without doubting! Beloved, YOU CAN!

Scripture for Meditation: Philippians 4:13; 2 Corinthians 12:9; Psalm 37:5 New International Version

Day 25

Faint Not!

Beloved, you must keep sowing your seeds. Stop worrying about what someone is going to give back to you. God didn't promise that the harvest would come from the same place that you planted the seed. His promise is that the harvest will come. You must be secure in the knowledge that God is not a man that He should lie, neither the son of man that He should repent. If the Lord said it, it will come to pass! Don't give up before your harvest comes. The promise is that we shall reap IF we faint not. You can't give up. Your harvest depends on you!

You may have slowed down. You may not be as excited as you were when you started out on your journey. You may even be feeling that you haven't accomplished much but God wants you to realize that you're not in the place that you started.

Examine the small steps you've taken and thank God for the progress that has been made. It's not over yet and there is more to come but how will you obtain it if you give up? Faint NOT! You can still finish strong! You can finish those projects! Keep working and believing and whatever you do, don't stop sowing! Your seeds have an appointed time and they will spring up IF you faint not.

Scripture for Meditation: Galatians 6:7-9 New Living Translation

Day 26

Why Me?

Somebody needs YOU! Many of you don't believe this because it appears that everyone is doing the same thing. Beloved, it's similar but NOT the same. You must know that you are uniquely created by God. Because of that, the results of what you do will uniquely impact that somebody that needs you!

Why me, you ask? It's simple. It has been planned for YOU! Nobody can do what God has planned for you to do in the way that God has planned for you to do it. I heard another woman of God say once- God has a plan and it includes you! You've been chosen for it!

Somebody needs the message that God has given you. Somebody needs the book that you'll write or the song that you'll sing. You have to remember that just because others do things that are similar to what you do, it doesn't meant it will have the same Impact.

You are the answer to someone's problem, dilemma or issue. You have the testimony that someone else needs to hear that will pull them through. And believe it or not, the very things that other people need, you need it also. What God uses to bless other people through you is also going to bless you. Beloved, you also have to do IT for YOU! It will never be ALL about you but YOU are included!

Scripture for Meditation: Jeremiah 29:11 New Living Translation

Day 27

Let God Do It in Your Life!

When God does it, the effects are irreversible! They can't be undone! Come hell or high water, troubles or tribulations, attacks and more, whatever GOD does in your life, NO ONE AND NO THING can undo it!

Today, on purpose, let God lead you into the direction that HE wants you to go. Let God show you what HE wants you to be and before you attempt to do it, let GOD DO IT! That means before you devise your own plan, seek Him for His plan. Before you take action, ask God what He wants you to do and how He wants you to do it.

He has promised to be there with you and He has already redeemed you! He has called you by your name says His Word. The waters won't drown you and the flames won't burn you up. The word says that you are HIS witnesses, the servants that HE chose!

Beloved, fear NOT! Be intentional and let God do it in your life! As the scripture said in Isaiah 43:13- When God acts, WHO can reverse it?

Let HIM DO IT!

Scripture for Meditation: Isaiah 43:1-13 New International Version

Day 28

Press In!

Today is a great day to press into your purpose. You must believe that your condition is not your conclusion. Where you started and how you started does not dictate where and how you will end. The pressure that you've experienced was necessary for the birthing of your purpose.

Don't allow what happened in the past or your current situation distract or discourage you from grabbing hold of your destiny. What God has planned for you will live. God wants you to believe HIM! Believe what He has said and live out your belief through your actions!

There is an expected end for you, a plan that will prosper and your future is still secure!

Beloved, I encourage you to make the decision to live with more hope today. God's purpose and plan is greater than your pressure and pain. Press in and don't lose hope!

Scripture for Meditation: Jeremiah 29:11 New International Version

Day 29

Refocus!

It's time to refocus your attention on the things of God. Often times you will get busy with the work and sometimes you may forfeit worship. I encourage you today to put your focus back on worship and fellowship with God. Yes, you must work but without worship, your work can be overwhelming and it could possibly be in vain.

Working the work WITHOUT the ONE who called you to it is dangerous. Where is your impact without the anointing? How do you produce fruit without the power of God working through you? You must spend time in His Presence to ensure that the work you are doing is His work, done His way and in His timing.

God knows that you have dreams. He allowed you to have them. But you must always remember that a dream is just a dream until the Dream Giver brings it to pass. God is the Dream Giver. Since only what you do for Christ will last, take a moment and refocus on HIM. Allow Him to guide you through the process of working what you're called to do!

It only takes a moment to refocus but the benefit will be lasting! Worship will help you to refocus our mind, heart and spirit on HIM and not IT.

Scripture for Meditation: Jeremiah 24:7; Jeremiah 29:13; Hebrews 12:1-2 New International Version

Day 30

Testify!

Do you realize that your life is a living, breathing, walking testimony to the redeeming power of Jesus Christ? Sometimes you may withhold your testimony out of fear of what people will think of your past. However, it could be your testimony that will cause someone to give their life to Christ.

There are other times that you withhold your testimony because you feel unqualified or you feel like you're still in the learning phase. Sometimes you have to pour out AS you're being poured into. Sometimes you have to share what you've learned while you learn more.

God wants you to know that there is drawing power in the testimony of what He has done IN you. Jesus told the woman at the well - "Indeed, the water I give them will become IN them a spring of water welling up to eternal life." What God has done in you, He desires to do in others. Your testimony can help draw them to Him. I urge you to allow what God has done to well up in you and overflow in your testimony as you share your new life and freedom with others.

Don't withhold your testimony. It may be the only thing that will draw someone else to Jesus. Don't withhold what Jesus has done for you and in you because somebody needs you. Only Jesus can save them but you and I can help to draw them. It only takes a moment to share something that can change somebody's life for eternity. Are you willing to allow God to use you and your testimony today? It may cause somebody else believe in and receive Jesus as their Savior! I encourage you to testify!

Scripture for Meditation: John 4:39-42 New International Version

Day 31

What Did God Say?

When you're in a press to do what God has called you to, don't allow what naysayers, counterfeit supporters or so called haters say to deter, distract or discourage you. It is extremely important that you remember what God has said about you. What God said overrules what anyone else can say, think or do! Beloved, the Word of God concerning you has more authority than any action of man!

Mans' "no" to you is simply the open invitation for Gods supernatural Yes. It's the time that onlookers will see the Glory of God revealed in you and in Gods call for you. It is the time that man will begin to understand what the scripture, "If God be for us, who can be against us," really means. God will prove His word through you!

Regardless of what man may say, keep what God has said about you in your heart and on your mind. Continue to speak it from your mouth! You have the power within you to speak what God has said. You have authority to live out what God has already called out! Don't settle, don't give up and always remember what God said! Hold fast to it and keep pressing.

Scripture for Meditation: Proverbs 4:23; Philippians 2:5; Jeremiah 1:9
New International Version

Day 32

Choose to Live for Him!

There is a benefit to walking upright and blameless before the Lord. We will never be perfect in the sense of getting it right all the time but we can strive daily to live holy and follow His commands.

In our submission to His will and our sincere efforts to live for Him, He pours out His wisdom to help us. He also gives us knowledge and understanding. The success that we desire will be found in our upright living. The protection that we need is attached to our blameless walk.

What does all that really mean? The Lord is not going to allow you to live for Him and not bless you. When you decide to live for Him, you also decide to be blessed by Him. He already has the blessings for your life stored up and ready to pour out on you. In fact, it will be His good pleasure to do so.

Live for Him and be blessed, protected, covered, shielded, and guarded by Him! It's your choice!

Scripture for Meditation: Proverbs 2:6-11 New International Version

Day 33

The Same Man - NOT the Same!

Have you ever experienced a time in your life that the change IN you caused people to ask the question - is that the same man or woman? It may be because what God did for you, through you and IN you literally made you unrecognizable. Don't worry, that's a good thing. It was done so that God could get more glory from your life. Some people may not believe or receive the change, but you can stand boldly and declare - *I am the same man but not the same!*

You can testify that you are the same man that used to be blind but now you see. You're the same man that used to be sick but now you're well. You're the same man that used to be a liar now you speak truth. You're the same man that used to be lukewarm but now you're on fire for God. You're the same man that USED TO but because He touched you now you are the same man but not the same!

Take joy knowing that some of what you've been through has not been because of any wrong doing on your part. It may not have been anyone else's fault either. It was most assuredly so that God could get the glory. Everything that you used to be is just that- what you used to be. God has made you better. God has made you over. God has made you stronger. God has made you wiser. It's our blessing that God has made us and not ourselves. So, do as Jesus instructed the blind man- GO! Go in what God has done in you! Go in what He has called you to. Again, some won't receive it, many won't recognize or acknowledge it but it doesn't mean that God didn't do it!

Scripture for Meditation: John 9:1-9 New International Version

Day 34

Not Yet!

We must learn to follow the example of Jesus! We must not allow people who don't even believe in us to push into places and things before it's time! You must be in relationship with Jesus so that you will know when it's your turn and your time!

Don't be swayed by the opinions of people or the "pushes" to move in a time that is not yours. Don't allow counterfeit supporters to cause you to go into the birthing room too soon or leap into a vision too early. Remember that Habakkuk said the vision is for an appointed time!

We must follow the example of Jesus. Sometimes we have to say-my time is NOT YET! That may mean that others will go before you. It may mean that others will leap first or jump in before you but it doesn't mean that you are not going. It only means - NOT YET!

I encourage you to do it in Gods timing and not man. Follow Gods leading and not man. Your time is fully coming. I pray that you'll wait on God to move you into it and don't allow man to push you prematurely!

Scripture for Meditation: John 7:1-8; Haggai 2:3
New International Version

Day 35

Identity Crisis!

In the midst of all those that are listed in the Scripture for Meditation and those who identified with a certain group, there were still some who "could not find their father's house or their genealogy."

Identity crisis didn't just begin. In this world that we live in, it's easy to feel like you can't find the place that you belong. Verse sixty-two says "These sought their listing among those who were registered by genealogy, but they were not found; therefore they were excluded from the priesthood as defiled."

Are you that person that has felt excluded? Have you felt like you don't belong? Have you searched for that place or group that you would fit into? It didn't matter where you were or who you were around, you always seemed like the odd ball.

In verse sixty-three, they were told that they shouldn't eat because of their "identity crisis." This is such a mirror of the world today! People will attempt to exclude you from their circles, cliques and even the Kingdom because you don't appear to fit. They may want to exclude you because you don't carry the name, title or etcetera that they may carry. Unfortunately, people will withhold the "food" that is needed to show you or guide you to your identity in Christ.

Just a thought to consider: The next time you encounter someone who appears to be different or doesn't fit in, don't withhold the word that they may need to resolve their identity crisis. Always remember that it could be you.

Scripture for Meditation: Ezra 2:59, 62-63 New King James Version

Day 36

Some People Ain't Never Satisfied!

Some people AIN'T NEVER satisfied! Look at Haman in the Scripture for Meditation! Do you know anyone like him in your life? Are YOU like him? Haman was bragging about all the good that he had. He boasted about his wealth, his many children, etc. But he counted it all as NOTHING because one man, Mordecai, wouldn't bow before him.

May I ask you today- what or who have you allowed to cause you to discount all the good in your life? What or who has that much control over your life that regardless of the many ways you are blessed, you STILL find that ONE thing that just makes you feel like it's still not enough?

Haman should truly make you check yourself. God has been too good. God has been too kind. Everything may not be as you'd prefer it to be. You may not have everything you desire and sometimes what you need but are you really going to allow those few things to outweigh all that God has done?

Haman gave Mordecai control over his life. Haman was evil and yes, he was plotting against Mordecai but it was Mordecai who was really in control. It was Mordecai that made Haman discount EVERYTHING good in his life. You've really got to put people, places and things in the right perspective. You cannot allow that ONE THING or that ONE PERSON to have so much control and influence over your life that you will negate every good thing that God has done and allowed in your life.

As I said, some people AIN'T NEVER satisfied! Don't let that be you today.

Scripture for Meditation- Esther 5:9-13 New Living Translation

Day 37

Choosing Differently!

Beloved, when you make covenants with others, you must know what you can and can't handle. Orpah, after hearing Naomi's words and what she would not be able to provide for her regarding another son to have as a husband, chose to take Naomi's blessings and go back to her homeland. Ruth on the other hand, decided differently. Her decision was to stay with Naomi and go wherever she went. They both knew what they could and could not handle.

It didn't mean that Orpah wasn't blessed, it just meant that she used wisdom to choose wisely and differently.

I love this scripture because Naomi had already spoken a blessing over both of them. They just chose to receive them differently. Orpah in going back and Ruth in staying with her.

What we can say about both women, is that they made an informed decision and regardless of which option they chose, there was a blessing spoken over them both.

I urge you to choose wisely, make informed decisions and don't judge others choices just because they choose differently.

Choosing differently does not always equate being wrong or outside of the will of God. We, as a people, have to do a better job of discerning the difference.

Scripture for Meditation: Ruth 1:11-14 New Living Translation

Day 38

It Takes More!

Beloved, it's time out! Decreeing and declaring, naming and claiming, spin around three times and jump up and down, slap your neighbor high five and take a victory lap- that's not going to get IT.

Whatever your IT is - it's going to take more! It's time out! And it's time IN!

You want more? You're going to have to do more. If you want it and you believe God for it then WORK FOR IT! Better yet, WORK for it and give God something to WORK with! Nothing from nothing is still nothing!

Everybody wants to put a praise on it but when will you put the WORK in on it?

It may not be easy but it will be worth it. It may not come immediately but it will come. It may not happen just as you plan but if the Lord said it, if the Lord commissioned you to It, WORK il and watch God work with you and for you.

Remember the scripture declares that faith without works is dead.

It's going to take more than believing, it's going to take work!

Scripture for Meditation: James 2:26 New Living Translation

Day 39

Keys to Answered Prayer!

Many times you will pray, pray, pray and pray some more but don't get an answer or you don't get the answer that you need or want. Here are some keys that will help you to see and receive answered prayer!

You must have faith in God. What is your faith level? Do you really believe God? You must really believe that it will happen. How many times have you prayed but not REALLY BELIEVED that God would do it? Do you believe that God will do what He said that He will do? Do you believe that God will do what you've asked Him to do? You must not have any doubt in your heart. Again, I ask, do you REALLY believe God and that He can and will do what you've asked of Him. Although this is hard sometimes, it's worth it to believe so that we can receive the answers.

You must also believe that you HAVE RECEIVED it. This is so key. You must believe that it's already yours. You have to believe that God has already done it for you in the spirit realm and that He will manifest it in the natural.

More importantly, you must forgive ANYONE that you are holding a grudge against. Before you do all those other things, FIRST you must forgive. Examine your heart and be honest because God already knows. Who is that person that you need to forgive? It doesn't matter who it is. Parents, children, spouse, family, friends - ANYONE. Forgive them.

I pray that you will acknowledge the instruction of the LORD and make the necessary changes so that you can live a life of ANSWERED PRAYER!

Scripture for Meditation: Mark 11:22-25 New Living Translation

Day 40

IF God Can...

How many times have you wondered IF God can? How many times have you doubted that God can or that God would? Remind yourself of the words of Jesus- "ANYTHING is possible IF a person believes."

Have you met a person that just believes that anything is possible? Maybe you're like the father in the reference, you believe yet there are times that you have to pray, Lord, help my unbelief.

Many of us have had those times. Maybe you're experiencing that right now? What area are you struggling with unbelief in? Is it yourself? Is it your vision or dream? Maybe it's your ability to live out the dream or vision.

As you look forward to the future, settle within yourself that GOD CAN in every area of your life. Ask the Lord to help your unbelief. Anything IS possible IF a person believes.

The IF doesn't belong with God, it's attached to us. If you can believe it, God has the power to do it!

Scripture for Meditation: Mark 9:22-24 New Living Translation

Day 41

JUST a Carpenter?

He's JUST a carpenter..... It is amazing that this is still the mindset of "believers" even today. The ironic part is that the "believers" are the ones who refuse to believe. I just want to encourage you - regardless of what you've been labeled as, know that God can use you. What you do doesn't necessarily define who you are. Just as there was much more to Jesus than JUST being a carpenter, there's much more to you.

Now, let me say this – there's absolutely nothing wrong with JUST being a carpenter. As Pastor E. Dewey Smith once said, what's wrong with a carpenter? What's wrong with being someone who builds? Isn't that what Jesus, our Savior, does? Why does it matter if He was a carpenter? It didn't mean that He was not the Savior.

God wants you to know that whatever you've been or whatever you've been labeled, it can't stop you from being who He birthed you in the earth to be.

People may question your wisdom. They may even question the power operating within you. They may talk about what you do, have done and where you come from. They may even refuse to receive, respect or believe in you but NONE of that will change the fact that you are who God sent you to be.

Just remember Jesus, "Just the carpenter" was so much more. So are you! Receive it! Be it! In Jesus Name!

Scripture for Meditation: Mark 6:2-3 New Living Translation

Day 42

It Must Be Carried Out!

What has Jesus required of you? What instructions has He given you that you have not completed? What have you tried to talk God out of because you didn't feel worthy or capable of doing it?

I believe that Jesus would answer you in the same manner that He did in the Scripture for Meditation and say "It should be done, for we must carry out all that God requires."

Whatever instructions you've received from the Lord, they must be carried out. It's not a matter of your inability, qualifications or even what people may think. What matters is following through on the things God has called you to.

Take a moment today to look back over some areas of your life that God has made a requirement or given you instructions but you have failed to carry out ALL that God required.

Make a decision today to agree with God concerning you. It must be carried out through you!

Scripture for Meditation: Mark 3:13-15 New Living Translation

Day 43

Be Consistent!

You must learn to be consistent especially when you are being attacked by the enemy. You must know that the work that has been assigned to your hands is too great to be stopped by distractions and attacks from outside sources and people. Too many of Gods people are entertaining the plots, attacks and distractions of the enemy and have lost focus of their assignment.

Inconsistency is one reason why the enemy feels like he can keep tempting you with the exact same thing. In the Scripture for Meditation, Nehemiah said "four times they sent me the SAME message and EACH TIME I gave them the SAME reply!"

Learn how to be consistent. Learn how to tell the devil no and stick to it. Learn how to let your yes be yes and your no be no in all things.

You must know that the work you're doing for the Kingdom whether it's in a ministry, the corporate world, a business venture or in your family - it's too great for you to come down. It's too great for you to just stop.

I encourage you to take inventory today and determine what areas you've slipped into inconsistency. Re-evaluate, regroup, refocus and be consistent!

Scripture for Meditation: Nehemiah 6: 3-4 New Living Translation

Day 44

New Seasons! New Horizons!

Consider today what time and season that you are in. Just as one month or day ends and a new one will begin, so are the things of your life. Allow what has been - the old things of the past to pass away from you and embrace the new that God has prepared for you. Letting go doesn't mean that you won't have anything. It signifies that you are ready to receive more! Just because you're letting go doesn't mean that something is wrong or something is not working. It simply means that time is up and the season has changed.

The question is - Will you change with it? OR Will you get caught in time?

The old days may have been great but greater is ahead of you! More is looking for you! While some things will transcend with you from one place to another, from one time to another, some things must come to an end so others can begin. Don't miss what God has for you by holding on to what's done. This may be your time to let it go and move on! That time has passed. That season is over! NEW is on the horizon for you!

Scripture for Meditation: Ecclesiastes 3: 1 New Living Translation

Day 45

Be Confident and Speak It!

In life - many times you may tend to second guess yourself. Sometimes you are unsure. Sometimes you feel inadequate. Other times you may feel that you won't be received but I encourage you to be confident!

You must be confident in what God has said to you. Be confident in what God has given you. Your gifts, talents, dreams and visions from God are enough for you.

Don't allow intimidation, fear, previous failure or people to shake your confidence or to drain it.

You have a promise from your great God that if you will decree a thing, it will be established for you. In other words, if you've got the faith and confidence to speak it, God has the power to perform it!

So, grab hold of your confidence, snatch it back if you have to and speak what you heard! Speak what you believe, work towards what you're speaking and watch God do it for you! Be confident and speak it! It will come to pass!

Scripture for Meditation: Job 22:28 New American Standard Bible

Day 46

LIVE!

There is life in you. I urge you to LIVE today! The word declares that "I shall not die, but live, and declare the works of the LORD."

There is work for you to do in this life! The works of the Lord are abounding everyday therefore every day of life that God gives you, there is a mandate on your life! That mandate is to LIVE and DECLARE!

Don't die in this season that God is calling you forth to live and live more abundantly! Don't give in to the things that are attempting to kill your dreams, steal your joy and destroy your destiny! The Word of God has already counteracted every attack of the enemy! Jesus, Himself has already cancelled every plan against you with His blood! He has given you all that you need to live and not die!

Speak the word over your life! I shall live and NOT die and declare the works of the Lord!

Once you speak it, do it! LIVE!

Scripture for Meditation: Psalm 118:17 New International Version

Day 47

How Long Will You Stay THERE?

Life throws you curve balls and most times you're not ready for them. Sometimes you endure hardships, heartbreak, pain, abuse, manipulation, loss and so much more. Even more, you hold on to these things as if they are your life treasures. Today, I ask you, how long will you stay THERE?

THERE is that place of bondage, that place of depression, anxiety, woe is me and most likely negative thoughts. THERE could be a place of hurt that you haven't yet forgiven and moved on from.

Would you take a moment now and examine your heart? Look over the things that you've been nursing and keeping alive that really need to be dead and buried. Ask yourself - which one is more important? The past or your future? What was done or what can you move on to do?

I encourage you to change the way you see those things. Yes, you were hurt, injured, broken or possibly abused but today you can look back and say "I lived THROUGH it." Those things didn't kill you back then. Why would you allow them to do so now?

God has such an awesome plan for your life. He has great things that He wants to do through you. It's time to embrace who you are in Him and make a decision to move forward. Don't live THERE anymore when your planned place of destiny is awaiting you!

Scripture for Meditation: Philippians 3:12-14 New International Version

Day 48

You Have What You Need!

God has given you everything that you need to accomplish what He sent you to do. The Word of God says that He has given you power and authority to drive out demons. What are demons? Evil spirits, sources of harm and distress.

Beloved, you must be reminded that no weapon formed against you shall be able to prosper. Regardless of what shape, form or fashion the weapon comes in - it has no ability. As a child of God, you are equipped with Gods power and authority! You already have within you everything that you need to win!

God wants you to proclaim the Kingdom of God and heal the sick. He wants you to share Jesus with the unsaved and the lost. Share the good news of the healing power of Jesus! Not just to the physically sick but to the spiritually sick and dead, you are to proclaim the power of the crucified and resurrected Savior. Your job is to make Jesus known! Make Him known through your conversation, make Him known through your actions and make Him known by the fruit that you produce and the love you show.

God has given you clear instructions. He has given you what you need and told you what you are assigned to do. Go forward and don't give up.

Scripture for Meditation: Luke 9:1-6 & 62 New International Version

Day 49

You Will Get To the Other Side!

When Jesus told the disciples "let us go to the other side," He never said that there wouldn't be trouble or adversity. He simply said "let us go to the other side." The blessing is that regardless of what came up on the way, they were going to get to the other side.

Beloved, storms are just things that have come up on the way. They are storms that you have to endure on the way to where God has promised. God wants you to be assured that you WILL get to the other side of this.

Just as the disciples lived through that storm, so will you live through this one! The storms that you encounter in life are not meant to take you out. They will test your faith. They will stretch your faith. Today, I pray for you as Jesus prayed for Peter that your faith will fail you not.

Jesus is not asleep concerning your storm, He's in it with you. Even if it appears that He's silent, He's still in it with you. Don't be afraid! Have faith and know that you will get to the other side!

Scripture for Meditation: Mark 4:35-40 New International Version

Day 50

The Authority of Yes and No! You Have It!

When someone adds you to a group that you don't prefer to be in on Facebook, you are presented with options. YOU have the authority on your end to choose what you'd like to do with those options.

One option is to click OK acknowledging that you've been added and you remain in the group.

Another option is to leave the group. Choosing this option only means that you could be RE-ADDED to the group without your permission or your desire to be in the group.

However, there is one last option that can be combined with the second option. Once you click leave group, the last option says- PREVENT OTHERS FROM ADDING YOU TO THE GROUP AGAIN.

Beloved, may I empower you today? Once you've left a person, place or thing - YOU have the authority to PREVENT OTHERS FROM ADDING YOU TO THEIR GROUP, ISSUE, PROBLEM, ETC. Stop letting people make you a part of something that you have no desire to be in OR that you're not GRACED to be in OR that your time IN is OVER and now you're OUT!

I encourage you to use your authority. That place, person or thing may not be for you anymore. If NO is your answer now, stick to it and don't be moved unless you are moved by God.

Scripture for Meditation: Matthew 5:37 New King James Version

Day 51

He Is Willing, Able and Waiting!

Do you know that Jesus is willing to heal you? You must not limit healing to your physical body. I encourage you to know and believe that He is willing to heal you in every area of your life. He is willing to heal your thoughts. He is willing to heal your mind. He is willing to heal your heart. He is willing to heal your brokenness. He is willing to heal your relationships. He is willing to heal your emotions. More importantly, God wants to heal your spirit man!

Many people have been hurt and broken at the hands of "church people." Those were the people that you thought should have understood. They may have been the people who said "I love you" in words but not in deeds. It could have come from people who simply didn't know how to handle you in the state or phase of life that you were in. It's okay! There is healing for your pain in every place that you hurt.

Jesus is the healing balm for all of your infirmities. His Spirit is liken unto a soothing salve that aids your discomfort. Not only is He willing and able to heal, He is waiting to heal you! Will you be the one to come to Him and receive today?

Scripture for Meditation: Matthew 8.1-3 New King James Version

Day 52

You Are A Winner!

Have you ever felt like the more you did right, the more things seemed to go wrong? The more you strive for excellence, sometimes it felt like you couldn't accomplish anything you set out to do? Every time you tried to do good - there was always something that happened opposite of what you were reaching for?

Those are simply distractions that were meant to keep you from reaching your goal. One of the enemy's main goals is to take your eyes off of Christ and divert your attention to the problem instead of the promise. Beloved, stand firm and do not be moved because the promise is still yours.

The enemy wants to discourage you and make you believe that you can't accomplish the goals you've set. He would like nothing more than to make you think that your dreams will not come to pass. This is why you should know that giving up now is the worst possible option. You are on the brink of everything you've worked and prayed for.

I encourage you to do as Apostle Paul said – "forget those things which are behind you and reach forward! Press toward the mark of the prize of the high calling in Christ Jesus." Don't give up because there is a blessing in your pressing and a reward for your faithfulness. I declare today that YOU are a winner!

Scripture for Meditation- Romans 7:9-25 The Living Bible; Philippians 3:13-14 New Living Translation

Day 53

Clean Out the Crevices of Your Life!

After you've spent time de-cluttering, it's necessary to clean out some things. The same is with your heart, mind & soul. Once you've sorted through your many emotions, thoughts and feelings, you must also release them.

Holding on to hurt and un-forgiveness creates a stronghold within you. God wants you to be free! Many people talk about living in victory daily but don't experience it because you have not cleaned out the crevices of your life. There is too much still lingering and laying about.

Maybe you're still replaying old, negative thoughts or hurtful conversations. Maybe you're still nursing an old wound that has closed and reopened because you won't let it go. Maybe you haven't forgiven YOU!

The bible teaches "So, if the Son sets you free, you are free indeed." Your freedom and victory is a matter of you letting go of the old and receiving what Jesus has completed at Calvary for you. God truly wants you to Live. In. Victory. Everyday! To do that, you must be free.

Clean out those crevices - the places that you know hurt and un-forgiveness is lingering and make a choice to let it go and move on. Be free in Jesus name!

Scripture for Meditation- Ecclesiastes 3:6 Message Bible
John 8:36 New Living Translation

Day 54

Watch and See!

I want to encourage those who have been petitioning the Lord. Maybe you've been fasting, praying, and waiting on the answer. Beloved, you must stay on your post and don't get out of position. God does have an answer for you. You've got to make a commitment to stick to it.

Habakkuk reminds us that we must keep watch over what we've prayed and asked God for. If you've never had a prayer journal, now is a good time to get one. Document your prayers, promises and even your complaints and keep watch to see. Part of your dilemma may be that you pray and forget what you prayed. This is the season that you need your eyes focused on what you've prayed about.

You may remember growing up and asking your parents for something, then telling your friends I asked my mama or I asked my daddy and I'm going to get it - watch and see. That's what I'm encouraging you to do - Watch AND See! You've asked your daddy - God. You've made your petition. You've circled the promises but beloved that's not all. You've got to stay in position. You've got to stay on your post and WATCH to SEE it! Be encouraged, not only will you see what the Lord will say, you'll see HOW the Lord will answer.

Scripture for Meditation- Habakkuk 2:1 Common English Bible

Day 55

You Must Keep Working To See It!

Sometimes you're the visionary and the runner. Most times when we read this reference scripture, we interpret this to mean that there are multiple people needed and required for the vision. However, sometimes it's YOU who has to read your vision and run with it.

It is necessary for us to write down what God has said to us and shown us. When you get weary while working the vision, it reminds you of the reason why you must keep working. When people don't hold up their end of the deal or don't do what's needed, it reminds you that God gave YOU the vision. When you feel like you don't have the money to do what's needed - read your own vision, reignite your own fire and run.

You're going to have to keep working to see what God said. You must keep working while you're waiting on answers. You've got to keep working even when it feels like God isn't going to answer.

Keep working!! You can't stop your work because your work is the evidence of your faith. Your work is the evidence that you're still on your post. Your work is the evidence that you're still in position. Your work says to God that you believe that you will see it! You've got to follow the instructions so you can possess the promise. Keep running!

Scripture for Meditation: Habakkuk 2:2 Common English Bible

Day 56

Get Back Up!

The steps of a good man are ordered by The Lord. A just man falls seven times.

Even when you fall or fail - your steps are still ordered by the Lord. If you feel like you've fallen, I encourage you to get back up. Get back up and try it again. Get back up and try something different, something new, but you can't stay down.

You were born to win and winners don't quit. You may lose sometimes. However, even when you lose, you still win. God has promised that all things work together for the good of them that love The Lord and are called according to His purpose. Getting back up requires you to believe what God has spoken about you.

Man may condemn you but God wants to convict you righteously. God wants to encourage you to get back up and into your rightful place in Him. Don't stay down because of the opinions of people when God has made a way for you to get up, get back to Him and be better in the end.

I encourage you to love God with everything you've got. Walk in the purpose He has called you to and even if you've fallen, today is your day - now is your time to Get Back Up!

Scripture for Meditation: Psalm 37:23; Romans 8:28; Luke 10:27
King James Version

Day 57

God Is Preparing You!

Whatever you're experiencing right now, it's part of your preparation process. In your process, you may experience a plethora of emotions. There may be highs and lows, depression, laughter, etc. Allow yourself time to process the process. Allow yourself time to learn from each place that you encounter.

In your preparation process, you must also keep in mind that God knew you. Jeremiah 1:5 states - "I knew you before I formed you in your mother's womb. Before you were born I set you apart and appointed you as my prophet to the nations."

Beloved, God knew who you would be before He formed you. He knew what you would and wouldn't do. He knew where you would fall and how it would happen. He knew everything about you before He formed you but He STILL formed you. You must also know that before you were born, God had already set your life in motion!

Be encouraged today knowing that wherever you are in life, God is preparing you for the next move, the next phase and the next thing that you are called to do. You may not be able to handle it right now but your preparation process is making you ready. And be encouraged believing that the preparation process is because God cares for you. He knows the plans He has for you and He has promised to complete what He started in you until the return of Jesus Christ.

Scripture for Meditation: Jeremiah 1:5; Philippians 1:6
New Living Translation

Day 58

As For Me!

There is so much going on in the world and even more importantly in the Kingdom of God. There comes a time when you must make a decision that is personal and purposeful. The writer in our Scripture for Meditation stated, "AS FOR ME, I look to the Lord for His help. I wait for God to save me; He will hear me."

When I read that, I decided that I am in agreement that AS FOR ME, I will look to the Lord not only for His help but His saving power, His grace and His mercy. I may fall but I decree that I will rise because the Lord will help me! Even when I've sinned and the Lord has to deal with me - AS FOR ME, I will look to the Lord for His help.

I would like to encourage you. It may look extremely bad right now and the enemy's hand may appear to be triumphing against you but look to the Lord for His help. You may have even backslidden into sin, into something you never thought you'd go back to but look to the Lord for His help. When YOU feel like where is God, remind yourself that He's in the same place that you left HIm but you can still look to Him for His help. Beloved, wait for God to save you because only He can!

Will you look to the Lord today? Will you wait for God to save you and believe that He hears you? I encourage you to pray against the spirit of heaviness and decide to put on your garment of praise. Allow your worship to lead you into a place of freedom and peace. Choose to believe that the help of the Lord is available to you!

Scripture for Meditation: Micah 7:7-10 The Living Bible

Day 59

You Better Watch!

If you've ever watched a Tyler Perry play or movie, you've heard the famous Madea say- "We Gotta Watch!" This statement is true even in the Kingdom of God. People will attempt to tell you anything and everything. If you're not watching, praying and studying for yourself, you will fall for it!

Beloved, God does not want you to just receive everything from everyone because many come with ill intentions. God's word is clear, we do NOT have to accept them just because they mention God or say the name Jesus. We all know that some of them are just lying! God has given us clear instructions in our Scripture for Meditation. If they don't believe what Christ taught, do NOT invite him into your home.

If you're wondering if you should or should not entertain someone on ANY level... friendship, romantic, business, ministry, etc., consider the Word of God- if they do not believe what Christ taught, if they are not speaking what Christ taught, If they are not living how Christ taught- DO NOT PARTNER WITH THEM!

But here's they key - you've got to WATCH! In order to watch effectively, to know whether or not what they say is truly what Jesus taught then you must know for yourself! That goes back to studying to show your own self approved and to know God's word for yourself. You can't watch if you don't know what you're looking for.

2 John 1:7-11 New Living Translation

Day 60

There is Hope! Restoration is Coming!

In the midst of all that is going on in this world, all of the things that call for the wrath of God to be unleashed upon the land, there is HOPE! It doesn't mean that God is not going to judge according to His word. He can't lie so He is going to do it!! However, God also has a plan for His faithful children.

God has a plan of restoration that He's waiting to share with His beloved sons and daughters. Take note of His word- I, GOD, will burst all confinements and lead them out into the open (MSG) and the Lord HIMSELF will guide you (NLT). That is good news to those who are striving to live holy, to walk upright and to live a life that is pleasing to the Master.

Allow Gods Word to be your encouragement to keep walking right. Keep living right even when living right seems like the hardest thing to do. Let Gods Word and the promises that He has made be your motivation and your daily fuel to stay faithful to Him!

What the Lord has said, He will do! There is Hope! Restoration is coming!

Micah 2:12-13 MSG Bible and New Living Translation

AUTHOR'S CONTACT INFO

Email:
LaTriceSpeaks@latricewilliams.com

Website:
www.latricewilliams.com

Facebook:
www.facebook.com/LaTriceWilliamsMinistries

Twitter/IG/Periscope:
Connect With Me @ LaTriceSpeaks

Other Books Available by LaTrice Williams
Hurt to Healing – The Book
Articles of Encouragement: 30 Days of
Empowering You!

www.ingramcontent.com/pod-product-compliance
Lightning Source LLC
Chambersburg PA
CBHW071430040426
42445CB00012BA/1324